Festivals

NEW YEAR

Alan Blackwood

A very old festival

Everybody celebrates New Year. Whatever other festivals and holidays we may enjoy, as Christians, Jews, Hindus, Muslims or Buddhists, we all observe New Year.

This fact is easy to understand. From the beginning of the very first civilizations, people have needed to record time. They have done this by noting the division between day and night (the Earth turning round on its axis); the regular waxing and waning of the moon (the moon moving round the Earth); or the apparently changing position of the sun in the sky through the seasons (in reality, the Earth moving round

The Ibo tribe in Nigeria celebrate New Year's Day.

the sun). From these observations they have plotted the passage of time from one year to the next. Celebrating the start of each new year seems a most natural thing to do.

The timing of the New Year, though, has varied among the peoples of the world. This has often depended on the use of a particular type of calendar – the plan or record of the year as a whole. Some races or civilizations have drawn up their calendar according to the phases of the moon (a lunar calendar). Some have done their reckoning by the sun (a solar calendar). Others have based their calculations on both (a lunar-solar calendar). We shall take a closer look at some of these calendars as we go along.

One other thing we shall notice is how often the same customs and beliefs occur among races and cultures that can have had little or no knowledge of each other. The hopes and fears that New Year brings seem common to nearly all of us.

In Hong Kong, peach blossom is believed to bring prosperity and good luck.

New Year festivals long ago

Ancient Egypt

Three thousand years ago, the Egyptians devised an excellent calendar. It was based on an event unique to their land – the annual rise and fall of the waters of the river Nile. Their astronomers observed that a certain star, Sirius, always appeared just before the waters rose. They therefore measured their year from one appearance of the star to the next, which worked out almost exactly the same as measuring it by the sun. It gave them a year of just over 365 days.

The symbol of Amon with Ankh (life) and the lions of past and future.

The appearance of the star, together with the flooding of the Nile, was also the obvious time to mark each New Year. In terms of our modern calendar this occurred about 23rd September. It was a good time to celebrate the New Year in other respects. The floods marked the end of one farming year and prepared the way for the next.

At their New Year celebrations the Egyptians honoured Amon, for many centuries the most important of their gods. His effigy, and those of his wife and son, were taken from the temple at Karnak and transported in decorated barges upstream to Luxor. The Pharaoh sat in his own royal barge. Priests and priestesses were in attendance and musicians filled the air with the sound of trumpets, drums and tambourines. Everybody watched this stately procession from the palm-fringed banks of the Nile.

When at last the month of singing, dancing and feasting came to an end, the sacred fleet made its way back to Karnak and the business of the year was resumed.

This painting in an Egyptian tomb at Luxor shows a harpist playing at a feast.

7

Babylonia

The kingdom of Babylonia flourished at the same time as the Egyptian civilization. It covered much of the region of Mesopotamia – a word meaning 'between the rivers', these being the Tigris and Euphrates, which flow into the Persian Gulf.

The Babylonian calendar, dating from about 2000 BC, was lunar-solar. It consisted of twelve months of thirty days each, reckoned by the moon; while the year as a whole was measured by the apparent progress of the sun above the horizon, from its lowest point to its highest point and back again. Because the total number of 360 days fell short of the length of a full year, an extra month was added every so often, to make up the difference.

For the Babylonians, spring was the time of their New Year. It was called the festival of *Akitu*,

A Babylonian calendar of lucky and unlucky dates.

and included a remarkable ceremony. Their all-powerful king was publicly stripped of his fine clothes by the high priests, and ordered to go away and humble himself before the gods. Meanwhile, laws were suspended, and people did more or less what they liked.

Three days later came a grand procession, in which the king reappeared in all his splendour. His authority was restored, and everybody – slaves, farmers, soldiers, shopkeepers, scribes – returned to their jobs and duties.

So, with each New Year the people of ancient Babylon really did start their own lives and the life of their community afresh.

A Babylonian king and queen celebrate at a garden banquet.

9

The Romans

Our word 'calendar' comes from the Latin *calendae*, meaning 'day of proclamation', when forthcoming events were announced. In the days of the Roman republic and empire, public announcements were made on the first day of each month.

For a long time, the first day of the whole Roman year was at the beginning of the month we know as March. But in 46 BC, Julius Caesar introduced a new and improved calendar – the Julian calendar – which measured the year strictly according to the sun, and divided it up into the twelve months now familiar to us.

The date of the Roman New Year was also changed, to the first day of Januarius (January).

This month was named after the god Janus, who was always portrayed with two faces, one looking back, the other looking forward in time.

The Romans celebrated their New Year, called the January *Calends* or *Kalends*, in grand style. It was closely linked to their other festival of *Saturnalia*, which corresponded to our Christmas time. They decorated their homes and exchanged presents, such as pots of honey to wish each other peace, and gold and silver to wish each other wealth. Many people also sent gifts to the emperor.

During the time of *Saturnalia* and the New Year, many laws were relaxed. Slaves ate with their masters, and people often dressed up in odd clothing – a festive practice which continues today in our New Year fancy dress parties.

Saturnalia *was a time when slaves and their masters ate and drank together.*

The Celtic festival of Samhain

When the Romans conquered Gaul (France) and a large part of the British Isles, during the period from about 100 BC to AD 100, they encountered the Celtic people. The Celts had their own very interesting culture. This included a festival called *Samhain* or *Sambain*, meaning 'summer's end'. It occurred at the end of our month of October, and was the Celtic equivalent of New Year.

At Samhain, *druids gathered mistletoe to keep ghosts away.*

At this time, druids, who were Celtic priests, formed an assembly and drew up new rules for the year ahead. They also practised divination, predicting events in the coming year, by such strange methods as examining the intestines of dead animals, or observing the flight of birds.

On the whole, the Celtic people took a rather gloomy view of their New Year, perhaps because winter still lay ahead of them. They believed *Samhain* was a time when the spirits of the dead returned to haunt the living. Druids went into the forests and gathered mistletoe, which was supposed to act as a charm against these ghosts. People joined hands and danced round bonfires, believing the flames would give them strength to live through the cold, dark months ahead.

Some of these ancient beliefs and practices have survived in our own Christmas celebrations, and in the festival of Hallowe'en, which falls on the last day of October.

A *Samhain* or Hallowe'en cake is fun to make and to eat with friends. It represents an ancient form of fortune-telling.

Add to the cake mix these objects: a ring (for marriage); a small coin (for wealth); a button or thimble (for a single or lonely life); a piece of rag (for poverty). Bake the cake, then share it out among friends. See who gets each of the objects hidden inside – and see whether it all comes true!

Jewish New Year

The Jewish calendar

The Jewish calendar (a lunar-solar one) has a long and quite complicated history. It dates back to around 1500 BC, when Moses led the Israelites out of Egypt and across the desert to Canaan, 'the land flowing with milk and honey'. He decreed a week of seven days, based on the length of each phase of the waxing and waning moon; and a year of fifty-two weeks, plus extra days as needed, so that the year did not lose time by the sun.

Moses gazes at 'the promised land'.

Most significantly, Moses declared the seventh day of each week a holy day, or Sabbath (which is a Saturday for Jewish people). He also decided that the New Year should start at the time of the autumn equinox.

Nearly a thousand years after Moses, the Israelites were captured by the Babylonians. The Babylonian calendar, as we have read on page 8, contained a year of twelve months, reckoned by the moon. The Israelites adopted this system of months into their own calendar, adding an extra month every third year, once again to keep it in step with the solar year.

The Jewish New Year now starts at the beginning of their month of *Tishri*. The date of this varies from year to year; but it still occurs around the time of the autumn equinox, as in the biblical days of old.

The departure of the Israelites from Egypt.

Rosh Hashanah

The Jews call their New Year *Rosh Hashanah*, and it marks the beginning of the holiest few days of their year. It is a time for repentance of sins and bad behaviour, and of a resolve to do better in the year to come.

At *Rosh Hashanah*, Jews everywhere attend services at their synagogue. A special feature of these services is the blowing of the *shofar*, a hollowed-out ram's horn. It is one of the most ancient musical instruments. According to the

A shofar is blown at Rosh Hashanah.

16

Old Testament of the Bible, Moses used a *shofar* to summon his people to hear the Ten Commandments; and it was also sounded at the famous battle of Jericho. People who are too ill to attend the synagogue at *Rosh Hashanah* sometimes ask to hear it blown in their own home, so sacred is its sound to them.

In more festive mood, Jewish children, like those of other faiths, are often given new clothes at New Year. Families sit down to a special *Rosh Hashanah* dinner. The table may be decorated with grapes, pomegranates and other seasonal fruits, to remind them of harvest time in biblical days. Loaves are baked, rounded rather like a snail's shell, to represent the year coming full circle. At their *Rosh Hashanah* dinner, Jewish people also eat honey, in the hope that the new year will be as sweet, and fish, which is a traditional Jewish symbol of plenty.

At New Year, Jews everywhere attend a service at a synagogue.

Muslim New Year

The religion of Islam uses a lunar calendar – one that follows the phases of the moon. This means that the number of days falls short of the year as reckoned by the sun. Unlike other calendars, the Islamic one does not compensate for this by adding extra days or an extra month every so often. Consequently, the months start eleven days earlier each year, and so, of course, does the New Year.

Muslims (followers of Islam) watch the sky for the new moon, which signals the start of the first month of *Muharram* and of New Year's Day. In the dry, clear atmosphere of North Africa and the Middle East, where many Muslims live, it is seldom missed.

On New Year's Day, Muslims everywhere read their holy book, the Koran. It tells how, in AD 622, the Prophet Muhammad fled from Mecca, narrowly escaping death. He was the founder of the Islamic religion, and this episode, called the *Hejira* ('The Flight'), marks the start of year one in the Muslim calendar.

In Egypt, the first sighting of the slim new crescent moon, from the tall minaret of a Cairo mosque, is greeted with much excitement. Children are given presents and new clothes. Wearing colourful dresses is a big event for girls, since for most of the year girls and women in strict Muslim families wear only dark-coloured garments.

A Cairo mosque and minaret.

Right *Muslims in Calcutta, India, celebrate the first day of* Muharram, *New Year's Day.*

18

New Year in Iran

Iran (formerly Persia) is a Muslim country, but it has long enjoyed its own special New Year festivities. These date back to pre-Islamic times, and they begin on the same day each year – 21st March.

In towns and villages the actual start of this New Year, called *Noruz*, is traditionally marked by the firing of a gun. But people prepare for the day well in advance. A week or two earlier they start to grow *sabzeh* (something you can try for yourself). They place grains of wheat, barley or some other cereal in shallow bowls of water, or lay them out on damp cotton wool. The grains soon sprout little green shoots, symbolizing spring and a new year of life and growth.

People also prepare a special New Year table display, which is believed to bring good fortune. It contains seven items whose names begin with the letter 's' in the old Persian language. These are: *sabzeh* (just mentioned); *sonbul* (hyacinth); *samanoo* (a type of sweet pudding); *serkeh* (vinegar); *senjed* (a type of olive); *sumac* (a local herb); and *seeb* (an apple).

The old Persian religion was Zoroastrianism, named after its founder, Zoroaster. Ahura Mazda was believed to be the supreme god. Those who followed this religion worshipped fire, and another custom of *Noruz* can be traced back to this. People light fires and jump over them, calling upon the flames to give them new life and strength for the year ahead.

An image of Ahura Mazda, dating back to about 400 BC.

Hindu New Year

Hinduism, the main religion of India, is thousands of years old, and its calendar still plays a big part in the lives of millions of Indian people. There are, in fact, several versions of this calendar. But for most Indian people, the Hindu New Year comes some time during the spring season.

The Tamils of southern India call their New Year *Varusha Pirappu* ('Birth of the Year'). They prepare for it by decorating their homes with fresh palm and mango leaves, and by sprinkling rice flour over the floors. They also believe it is very important that when they wake on New Year's Day, the first thing they see should be something beautiful and good. So they often sleep by their family shrine, garlanded for the occasion with flowers and fresh fruit.

In the neighbouring south Indian state of Kerala there is a similar custom. Mothers prepare a 'tray of plenty', with food, flowers and little tokens of gold. On New Year's morning, children are told to keep their eyes closed, and not to open them until they have been led to the tray.

The Bengalis living in the north-east Indian state of West Bengal love to deck themselves with flowers, especially pink, red, purple and white blossoms – colours associated with the various Hindu gods and goddesses. Bengali women also like to wear something yellow to symbolize spring.

Bengali women like to decorate themselves with flowers – yellow symbolizes spring.

21

As a good luck charm, Bengali people place an earthenware pot, marked · with the ancient religious sign of the swastika, in front of their homes. They fill it with holy water, and put in a small branch from a mango tree.

In the large central Indian state of Maharashtra, they call New Year's Day *Gudhi Padwa*, or 'flag flying day'. Saffron-coloured flags flutter from all the rooftops and some people also hoist their own gaily-coloured silk head-dresses. Saffron, a strong orange colour, has a special meaning in both the Hindu and Buddhist religions.

To the north-west of Maharashtra, the Gujarati people have a distinctive cultural life of their own. They celebrate their New Year at the end of October, combining it with another important Indian festival called *Diwali*.

A Raja in his court celebrates Diwali.

Indian families make Diwali *lamps, using clay bowls in which they place oil and a wick.*

Diwali means 'cluster of lights'. It describes the age-old custom of lining the parapets of buildings with thousands of small, glowing oil lamps. Clusters of these lamps are also floated on rivers and lakes, where the water adds to their sparkle.

Nobody is sure what first inspired this festival. Some say it celebrates events in a great Hindu epic poem called the *Ramayana*. In this, the god-like hero, Prince Rama, is exiled from his own land. After fourteen years he returns home to become king and the people are so pleased that they light lamps to welcome him. Another story from the same epic relates how Rama fought and defeated a terrible demon king, so saving mankind from destruction.

The thousands of lights glowing and flickering through the night certainly create a magical atmosphere. For the Gujaratis they make a delightful start to the New Year.

New Year in the Far East

In Laos, Kampuchea, Burma and Thailand, the people are nearly all Buddhist, but many of them still observe the Hindu New Year. They make it a time to wash their beautiful statues of the Buddha with scented water. Or they throw buckets of water over each other, first colouring the water with dyes. They believe these actions will ensure a

These Burmese girls are throwing water over each other as part of the New Year water festival.

good rainy season, bringing welcome relief from the heat and dust that precede the rain.

One special custom is that of freeing pets, such as birds and fish. An unusual version of this custom concerns turtles. People buy a live turtle from market a few days before the New Year itself. They stick pieces of gold paper on to the creature's thick, horny shell and then release it on New Year's Day. These acts of kindness are believed to be rewarded with both luck and prosperity in the year to come.

On the island of Sri Lanka (formerly Ceylon), the people are mostly Singhalese, who are Buddhists; or Tamils, who are Hindus. But both share many of the same New Year traditions. They take a lively interest in astrology, and newspapers, radio and television are full of predictions for the year ahead, taken from the Hindu almanac. Sri Lankans also decorate their homes, using the lucky colour for the year.

You can make scented water, by soaking certain flowers, leaves, herbs and spices in very hot water. Try lavender, rose petals, cloves or nutmeg. When you have made individual scented waters, try mixing them to produce more interesting aromas. Scented waters can be stored for a short time in air-tight jars.

For the islanders of Sumba, in Indonesia, the New Year is marked by the arrival of nyale worms in the sea in February or March. This is immediately followed by the *Posola* festival, which involves ritual fighting on horse-back with blunted spears. Its origins are in the old belief that shedding blood will ensure the fertility of the earth in the year ahead.

The Posola *festival on the island of Sumba in Indonesia.*

The Chinese calendar

The Chinese calendar goes back in time to at least 1500 BC. It is lunar-solar, its months being reckoned by the moon, while the year as a whole is measured by the sun. An extra month is added at regular intervals to keep the two systems of measurement in line. The Chinese New Year coincides with the new moon, some time between 21st January and 19th February.

The Chinese name each year after an animal. An amusing legend relates that the creatures

Animal years

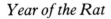

Year of the Rat

Rats are supposed to sleep by day and search for food at night. So people born in the daytime will have an easy life, while those born at night will work hard.

Year of the Ox

Patient and thoughtful, tries hard at things and does not give up easily.

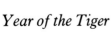

Year of the Tiger

Loyal to friends and a good provider for the family.

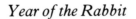

Year of the Rabbit

Happy and contented, and probably blessed with a large family!

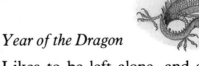

Year of the Dragon

Likes to be left alone, and objects to too much change. Fond of the night-time.

Year of the Snake

Wise and agile. Versatile and good at many things.

concerned agreed to have a swimming race across a river to decide whose year should come first. The rat won, because he cunningly jumped on the back of the ox, who was the best swimmer among them, and then leapt ashore at the last moment.

There are twelve animals involved, their year coming round again in a regular cycle. As the legend suggests, each cycle starts with the Year of the Rat. Then come the years of the ox, tiger, rabbit or hare, dragon, snake, horse, ram, monkey, cock, dog, and pig.

Year of the Horse

Strong and friendly and gets on well with strangers.

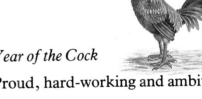

Year of the Cock

Proud, hard-working and ambitious.

Year of the Ram

Proud, but good at leading and helping others.

Year of the Dog

Loyal, like the tiger, and quick to learn, like the monkey.

Year of the Monkey

Very curious and quick to learn. Makes a good parent.

Year of the Pig

Very intelligent, but also emotional and easily upset. A good parent.

People are supposed to have the characteristics of the animal in whose year they were born – just as they are according to the twelve signs of the zodiac. On pages 28 and 29 you can see what these characteristics are. Note that in recent times, the years of the rat have been 1960, 1972 and 1984, so you can easily find out which year and animal applies to you and your friends.

Chinese celebrations

The Chinese New Year, called *Yuan Tan*, is celebrated by Chinese people everywhere. It is regarded as everybody's birthday, no matter what their actual date of birth might be. A person born only the day before is still considered to be one year old on New Year's Day.

The Chinese long believed that at New Year all the gods reported to the ruler of heaven – the Jade Emperor – about the happenings of the past year. To this day, Chinese children burn a little paper image of their family or 'kitchen' god, believing he will rise up to heaven in the smoke and make his own report.

Chinese New Year celebrations in Sydney, Australia.

Another age-old belief is that evil spirits are about at New Year. Firecrackers are supposed to drive them away. Families sometimes seal the doors and windows of their homes with strips of red paper (red is a lucky Chinese colour) to keep out bad spirits, before sitting down to their special New Year meal. This usually includes dumplings with nuts and sugar, which symbolize a happy and prosperous family life.

Most spectacular are the Chinese New Year street processions, illuminated by lanterns. These always include a fabulous Chinese dragon – symbol of strength and good luck – with bulging eyes, gaping mouth, and a body made from lengths of bamboo covered with coloured cloth or paper. Some dragons are over 30 metres (100 ft) long and require fifty or more people to keep them twisting and turning through the streets. There are musicians, dancers, clowns and often an acrobat dressed up as the comical, lovable old Chinese lion, *Sze Tse*.

The Lion Dance, taking place in Hong Kong.

The Vietnamese Tet Festival

Vietnam is next door to China, and joins in the Chinese New Year, which the Vietnamese themselves call the *Tet* festival.

The Vietnamese, like the Chinese, also believe in a 'kitchen' god – a sort of personal god attached to each household – who at the time of New Year is supposed to report to heaven on how the family has behaved during the year. According to their mythology, the kitchen god travels to heaven on the back of a large carp, a type of freshwater fish. Some Vietnamese households still honour this tradition by buying a carp in the market a few days before the start of the *Tet* festival, placing it in a large bowl of water before the family shrine, then releasing it into a local river or pond on the first day of the festival itself.

The Vietnamese buy a carp and release it on the first day of the Tet *festival.*

By a fascinating coincidence, the Vietnamese have another New Year tradition very similar to one still practised by many Scottish people. They believe that the character of the first person to step across the threshold of their homes at the start of the festival will influence their lives for the coming year. So they try to arrange beforehand for it to be someone they like and who will bring them good fortune.

For thousands of years both the Chinese and Vietnamese people have had great respect for their ancestors. Yet another of their New Year customs is to make paper money and burn it, as an offering to their ancestors in heaven.

Chinese and Vietnamese people burn paper money as an offering to their ancestors.

New Year in Japan

The Japanese New Year, or *Gan-Tan*, is now celebrated on 1st January. It is in many ways similar to the New Year holiday in the United States and other Western countries.

But the Japanese people like to keep up some traditional customs, connected with their age-old Shinto religion. One of these is to hang a kind of rope across the front of their homes, to keep out evil spirits. Called a *shimenawa*, it is made from rice straw and decorated with strips of white cloth.

At New Year it is customary for Japanese to dress in kimonos and pray at their local shrine.

Hmong New Year

Another remarkable kind of rope plays a part in the New Year of the Miao or Hmong people, who once lived in southern China, and are now scattered over much of the Far East, as far afield as Australia.

They too have an ancient fear of bad spirits at New Year, and an extraordinary way of dealing with them. First, they sweep up all the dust, dirt and soot from their homes, in which bad spirits like to live. Then they tip it beside a rope which has been slung round a tree to make a large loop. Finally, they jump through the loop several times in each direction. The bad spirits come out of the dust and try to follow, but soon get confused by all the jumping to and fro, and give up the chase. In this way the Hmong people believe they enter each New Year free from the old year's evil and bad luck.

A Miao or Hmong New Year game has two rows of children facing each other. They begin throwing a large, soft ball to and fro between them. There need be no strict order to this. Anyone who lets the ball drop must pay some forfeit, for example, sing a song, recite a poem, or give the person who last threw the ball some small gift.

New Year in the West

Julius Caesar reformed the Roman calendar, measuring it against the yearly movement of the sun, and making the first day of January the first day of the year.

Unfortunately, his astronomers were not quite accurate in their calculations. They estimated the whole year to be a few minutes longer than it really is. So, as time went by, the days and weeks drifted further and further away from their due season of the year.

This error was finally corrected in 1582, when Pope Gregory XIII introduced a revised version

This procession is part of the Tournament of the Roses festival, held annually in Pasadena, California.

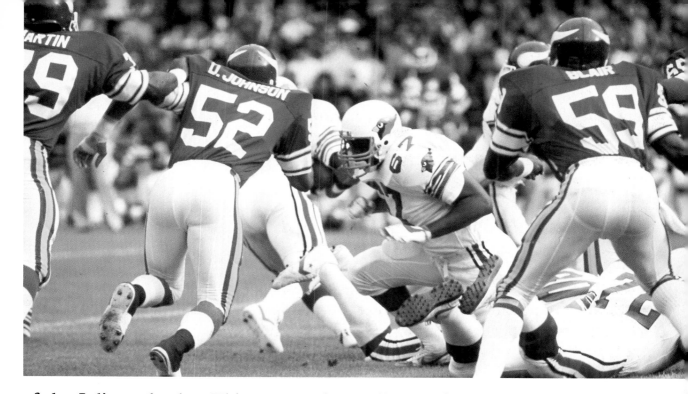

of the Julian calendar. This new version, called the Gregorian calendar, was gradually taken over by most of the countries of Europe.

Its use also spread across the world, as European nations, notably Britain, France, Spain, Portugal and Holland, created new colonies and empires, in the Americas, in Africa and the Far East. Great new nations, such as the United States of America, then Canada, Australia and New Zealand, also adopted it.

The Gregorian calendar gives us the dates for Christmas, Easter and the other Christian festivals, national holidays (for example, American Independence Day on 4th July), and, of course, our New Year's Day on 1st January. This is the New Year that nearly everyone around the world now recognizes; though, as we have seen, millions of Hindus, Chinese, Jews, Muslims and others still celebrate their own New Year as well.

The Tournament of the Roses ends with a football match at the Rose Bowl Stadium on New Year's Day.

Superstitions

The Gregorian New Year is not such a strongly religious occasion as some of the other New Year festivals we have read about. But many fascinating old beliefs and superstitions are connected with it.

In parts of the British Isles there used to be a tradition of 'drawing first water' very early on New Year's Day. Children fetched water from a well and went around sprinkling it on people and homes, to bring good luck.

German girls used to try and foretell the future by dropping molten lead into cold water.

A young girl sleeps with ivy under her pillow, hoping to dream of her future husband.

In Germany, an old New Year custom was to drop lumps of hot, molten lead in a bucket or barrel of cold water. As the pieces of lead cooled and hardened, people examined their shape. A round ring shape signified a wedding. If they thought the lead looked like a ship, this foretold a journey. In England, girls used to drop the white of an egg into water. The egg-white, they hoped, would form the initial letter of the name of the man they were going to marry.

For many people, dreams have had a special significance on New Year's Eve. In Ireland, girls slept with a sprig of mistletoe, holly or ivy under their pillow, believing they would dream of their future husbands. In Greece, it was once the New Year custom for girls to eat something salty just before they went to bed. As they slept they would get thirsty, and dream of a man bringing them water to drink. That man would turn out to be their future husband.

In the Appenzell area of Switzerland, people still dress up in fantastic costumes on St. Sylvester's Eve.

St. Sylvester's Eve

Several Christian saints play an important part in New Year celebrations. One is St. Sylvester, who became Pope in AD 314, just at the time Christianity became the official religion of the Roman Empire.

A New Year legend tells that he captured and imprisoned a huge and terrible sea monster called Leviathan. Though the people thanked God for this, they believed that on New Year's Day in the year 1000, Leviathan would escape again and destroy the whole world.

When a new Pope, also named Sylvester, was installed in the year 999, people remembered the legend and were terrified of what might happen. But when, on the first day of the year 1000 Leviathan did not appear, and the world did not come to a dreadful end, everyone rejoiced.

Since then, New Year's Eve has also been known as St. Sylvester's Eve in parts of Europe. In some Swiss and Austrian townships, people still commemorate the legend by dressing up in weird, fantastic costumes and parading through the streets. They call themselves *Sylvesterklauses* – 'Sylvester's hermits' – and they represent the demons who served Leviathan, and the angels, who aided St. Sylvester in his victory.

It is interesting to note that this colourful event takes place on 13th January, which was the date of New Year's Day according to the old Julian calendar we have read about on page 10.

Sylvesterklauses wear bells of all sizes and ingenious head adornments.

41

The Greek Festival of St. Basil

In Greece, New Year's Day is also the Festival of St. Basil. He lived from about AD 330 to 380, and was one of the founding figures of the Orthodox Church.

St. Basil was well-known for his kindness and generosity, and for many Greek children he is their equivalent of Father Christmas. Children leave their shoes by the fireplace when they go to bed on New Year's Eve, hoping that St. Basil will fill the shoes with gifts.

Another Greek tradition at New Year is to bake *Vassilopitta,* or St. Basil's cake. It is the custom

St. Basil.

for the head of the household to cut the cake, putting aside the first piece in remembrance of the saint himself. The cake should contain a ring or gold coin. Whoever finds this in their portion will have a lucky year. At one time it was also the custom to leave a piece of cake for the family donkey, goat or other livestock.

The *Vassilopitta* celebrates the legend about St. Basil. It relates that during his lifetime, the people had no money to pay their taxes. To try and save them from punishment, St. Basil collected from each some personal item, such as a ring or piece of jewellery. These he presented to the local governor, who then felt so sorry for the people that he asked St. Basil to return everything. The saint could not remember who owned what, so he put them all into loaves of bread. When the bread was distributed, each item miraculously found its way back to its owner.

An old Greek custom was to save a piece of Vassilopitta *for the family donkey.*

Hogmanay

New Year means something special to the Scots. They call it Hogmanay, a word which may come from an old French expression to do with lucky mistletoe.

At Hogmanay, it is the custom in many Scottish towns and villages to roll a blazing tar barrel through the streets, burn an old boat, or a straw figure called 'The Auld Wife'. These actions symbolize the burning up of the last remains of the old year, to make way for the new.

In Scotland people still observe many old superstitions connected with Hogmanay. One of these is called 'first-footing'. Scots believe the first person to enter their homes on New Year's Day can influence the year ahead, for good or ill. Dark-

Piping in the haggis.

First-footing.

haired men are a good omen, especially if they are carrying a lump of coal for the fire. Flat-footed people are considered very unlucky visitors.

One Hogmanay custom that is now world-wide is the singing of *Auld Lang Syne* at the stroke of midnight on New Year's Eve. The idea of having everybody stand in a circle and join hands as they sing probably comes down to us from the ancient Celtic practice, described earlier, of dancing round bonfires at the festival of *Samhain*.

On 25 January Scots celebrate Burns' Night in honour of the Scottish poet Robert Burns. Parties are held at which it is traditional for a piper to 'pipe in' the haggis (a kind of meat and oatmeal pudding cooked in a sheep's stomach).

Acknowledgements

The publisher would like to thank all those who provided pictures on the following pages: cover by courtesy of the Austrian National Tourist Office; Australian Information Service, London 30; British Tourist Authority 45; Camerapix Hutchinson Library 4, 5, 24, 25, 27, 33; Camera Press 16; Bruce Coleman (M. Freeman) 19, (Hans Reinhard) 32; Bill Donohoe 13, 26, 35, 39, 43; Mary Evans Picture Library 14, 38, 42; Hong Kong Tourist Association 31; The Mansell Collection 11, 15; Wendy Meadway 28, 29; Ann & Bury Peerless 22, 23; Peter Newark's Western Americana 12; Outlook Films Ltd. 7, 18; PHOTRI 17, 36; Rex Features Ltd. 37, 40, 41; Scottish Tourist Board 44; Ronald Sheridan's Photo-Library 6, 8, 9, 10, 20; TOPHAM 34; Wayland Picture Library 21.